ARCHITECTURE & DESIGN LIBRARY

FRENCH COUNTRY

ARCHITECTURE & DESIGN LIBRARY

FRENCH COUNTRY

Barbara Buchholz and Lisa Skolnik

FRIEDMAN/FAIRFAX

PUBLISHERS

A FRIEDMAN/FAIRFAX BOOK

© 1996 by Michael Friedman Publishing Group, Inc.

Library of Congress Cataloging-in-Publication data available upon request.

ISBN 1-56799-254-4

Editor: Hallie Einhorn
Art Director: Lynne Yeamans
Photography Editor: Wendy Missan
Production Associate: Camille Lee

Color separations by Bright Arts Singapore Pte. Ltd.
Printed in the United States

For bulk purchases and special sales, please contact:
Friedman/Fairfax Publishers
Attention: Sales Department
15 West 26th Street
New York, New York 10010
212/685-6610   FAX 212/685-1307

C o n t e n t s

INTRODUCTION

Nothing conjures up the notion of French country style more vividly than the vignettes that have been etched in our memories over the years, gleaned from sources as varied as our travels, foreign films, restaurants, and the works of renowned artists.

Sometimes, just one element is enough to immediately suggest French country design. Picture a pair of handmade white lace curtains that cover multipaned windows through which bright sunlight streams from an azure sky. Or, imagine a Louis XV walnut armchair with hand-carved slats and woven rush seats. An imposing armoire with paneled double doors and intricate carvings covering its richly burnished cherry exterior also conveys a French impression.

In other instances, the effect is carried out by an entire roomful of elements that work together to embody the French country mood. Envision a large country kitchen with colorful tiles hiding crusty stone walls, a long wooden harvest table surrounded by mismatched chairs, an antique cooker adjacent to a working fireplace providing physical warmth, and an array of copper pots suspended from a ceiling rack and gleaming overhead. A living room graced with a magnificent old hearth, worn ceiling beams, and a stone floor can exude an equally classic French ambience, particularly when the upholstery consists of tiny provincial prints.

The best part about French country style is that no single ideal truly defines it. France is the only country in Western Europe that belongs to both the northern and southern portions of the continent, resulting in a wide diversity of design and architectural elements. Each of the provinces, and even many of the towns within a particular province, has its own colloquial style. All these regional characteristics contribute to the common vernacular that has come to be known as French country style.

In Brittany, a northwestern province popular for country getaways, old houses in myriad configurations (from small manors—the two-room dwellings dating from the sixteenth century that first allowed a family and its domestics to have their own spaces—to farmhouses and row houses built to house several families around communal fields) are constructed from indigenous granite and topped with tufted thatch. In Normandy, just northwest of Paris, charming half-timbered structures

OPPOSITE: *The Rhone river flows through the gentle landscape of southeastern France, making it a fertile farming region. Among the region's crops is lavender, which lends its evocative scent to perfume.*

ABOVE: *Much of the charm of French country style lies in the attention to detail that is so typical. Here, potted plants and a window box bring warmth and color to the façade of an ivy-draped home, while sunshine peeks through the lace-curtained second-story window.*

faced with clay and punctuated with steeply sloped roofs prevail. In Alsace, at the far northeastern border of the country, the same materials have been used to produce houses that are heavily ornamented with colorful hues and gingerbread trims, reminiscent of nearby Germany.

To the south, the same kind of diversity reigns supreme. Large whitewashed dwellings with canal-tiled roofs dot the Basque landscape in the western part of the region. These homes were often built three stories tall to house a cart shed on the first floor, the living quarters on the second floor, and a balconied attic, where harvests were stored and clothes were hung to dry in the open air, on the top level.

Provence, perhaps most famous as the standard bearer of the French country style, is located in the southeastern portion of France, and its homes exude a Mediterranean flavor. The exteriors of limestone rubble structures are smoothed down and drenched in earth tones that reflect the cheerful countryside. Produced from oxides in the local sand and rocks, such hues as rose, ocher, wisteria, and sienna adorn the otherwise plain façades and are punctuated by contrasting colors used on the shutters. Over time, the sun bleaches the colors to more subdued tones.

Inside the abodes, local construction styles are equally distinct, for they are highly dependent on the modest materials native to the particular region. Although many of these architectural elements were originally designed primarily with the intention of providing structural support, they also serve as stunning decorative details. For instance, a beamed and trussed ceiling is a breathtaking sight that radiates old-world charm, but such a ceiling was actually designed because it offered the sturdiest and most sensible construction technique. The joists and supports were traditionally crafted of local timber, with many retaining their natural curves since entire trees sometimes were used at one time. The treatment of the timbers varied by region; some were left natural, while others were whitewashed or stained with walnut oil for a richer look.

Fireplaces and hearths, which served as the original center of the home because they were used for heating the household and cooking, also reflect regional differences. Some were built with niches set into the wall to provide extra storage; others had benches off to one side for resting by the fire. The most imposing were built in dressed stone, though most were constructed of simple rubble, which ages gracefully.

Walls were constructed of the same materials as the exterior of a structure. They could be timbered and filled in with lime or mud plaster, or they could be made of brick. Floors often consisted of flagstones or brick in northern France and clay tiles in the South.

LEFT: *The past is ever present at this warm-hued Alsatian farm-house, where a creative gardener has transformed an old well into a unique planter, brimming with colorful blooms.*

T O P : *Plentiful and enduring, limestone was a major building material in the south of France. Here, in the town of St. Jeannet, a doorway dating to 1834 is set into the limestone façade.* A B O V E : *A delightful farmhouse in Normandy features the half-timbered construction and thatched roof that are so typical of this region.*

Just as the architectural components of various regions are distinct, so too are the furnishings, though they bear striking similarities in their general forms and functions. There are a couple of aspects that account for the parallels. First, French country furnishings were made,

primarily, to serve specific needs that people throughout France shared. Thus, the same types of pieces are found throughout all the regions, though these pieces differ in ornamentation.

Second, the styles that slowly seeped into the provinces where working-class people lived came from the same sources—the courts of such design tastemasters as King Louis XIII and King Louis XV (the latter having had the greatest impact on French country design). As styles traveled to the different regions after decades of popularity among the wealthy, they were slightly altered to suit the particular climate, geography, and financial resources.

Thus, a *dressoir* (a buffet topped with rows of shelves) would be decorated in a spare manner if it was made in Auvergne in central France, but would have intricately carved details if it were crafted in Normandy. In Brittany, turned spindle plate guards would embellish shelves, while painted flowers would enhance an Alsatian piece. Beds were totally enclosed by richly carved wooden panels in Brittany, semi-boxed and hung with drapes in Normandy, and made with four short posts, then draped with canopies, in the South.

Further differences in style arose from the preferences of individual craftsmen, how much or how little embellishment they favored, and their degree of skill. In fact, it is the individual interpretations and the odd or eclectic details that worked their way into country pieces, rather than any literal copying of high styles, that give French country furnishings their true charm and charisma.

Today, the French country look is coveted for its casual elegance and originality. Ironically, though, this much beloved style defies the notion of decorating as we know it, since it evolved, for the most part, from working-class roots. Many individual pieces may be quite magnificent and grand, but these were often commissioned for special occasions, such as weddings, where specific pieces were given as part of a dowry. Granted, as the population living in the countryside became more affluent in the nineteenth cenury, more pieces were made and the trappings of decor, such as wall and floor treaments, became more

ABOVE: *Roofs of terra-cotta tiles characterize the venerable dwellings found in the oldest section of this quintessential Provençal town.*

refined. But this is a style that evolved from the realities of country life, and as such does not need to be strictly confined.

Thus, bringing the French country style into our homes does not require a perfect duplication of the elements, for there were few, if any, hard and fast rules to begin with. Furthermore, every single element need not be ostensibly French country. An individual piece—be it a distinguished French armoire or simple harvest table—can work beautifully with furnishings from other countries as well as with traditions that are older or more modern.

In the following pages, we will examine the individual components and rooms that best define the French country style, as well as the exteriors and their settings. Each of these aspects has the almost magical power to create a mood that unmistakably spells *la belle France.*

CHAPTER ONE

THE OUTSIDE VIEW

Throughout France, the homes and landscaping reflect the geography, climate, and natural resources of the province in which they are situated. Hence, the regional, or vernacular, designs that have emerged over time are as distinct in France as they are in the United States, where narrow townhouses rise vertically in the urban centers of the Northeast to compensate for the scarcity of land and where mansions with immense porches proliferate in the deep reaches of the South.

In rural areas of Normandy, where wood has traditionally been plentiful, timber-framed buildings are commonplace. In Brittany, modest farmers would construct thatched or stone houses, which they shared with family members and animals. Wooden chalets with sloping roofs were designed to protect occupants and the structures themselves from heavy rains in the mountainous Alps. And in Provence, inhabited long ago by Romans, clay tile roofs in different hues have dotted the landscape for centuries.

At the same time, similarities have abounded and continue to be present. Throughout France, in both cities and the countryside, homeowners share a deep love for their abodes and pay great attention to the choice of architectural details, such as the windows, doors, and trim, as well as to the colors used to enhance the façades. They eagerly call upon their own skills or those of their area's craftspeople—the thatcher, brick maker, stone mason, carpenter, and gardener—to make the exteriors of their homes as enticing as the interiors.

OPPOSITE: *The rough-cut stone street and the half-timbered home with a brick foundation are typical of Normandy, where the wooded countryside traditionally offered a rich source of timber for construction. Sometimes the timbers were laid in a diagonal display to show the craftsperson's skill and artistic bent. Thatched roofs, once common, gave way to slate in the nineteenth century, as slate was sturdier, more fire-resistant, and provided a more dignified demeanor.*

LEFT: *French country cottages often put on a painted face. Their owners either completely cover the surface of the structure with pigment, or simply focus on the building's prominent architectural elements, making them even more eye-catching by painting them in bright hues. Here, cream-colored limestone bricks are left in their natural state, but the characteristic Mediterranean windows and doors, which tend to be narrow, deep, and flanked by slat-board shutters, are painted a clean sky blue. Red and pink flowers, lush foliage, and lace curtains are additional characteristically French elements.*

RIGHT: *In Nice, homes are painted brilliant colors with pigments made from local rocks. The paints not only dazzle the eyes, but waterproof the exteriors as well. With deep crimson walls and turquoise blue louvered wooden doors, this home is a vivid example. The white frames around the doors and the lacy wrought-iron detailing, which has a Spanish feeling, make the crimson and blue even more prominent. With time and sunlight, the bright colors will weather to a softer palette.*

OPPOSITE: *There are many ways in which the French introduce a welcoming feeling to the home. In this case, the feat is accomplished by trellised plants climbing along the window-framed front door, two pots housing rose bushes that add color and fragrance, and foliage that softens the brick walkway. But the handmade lace curtains, known as* dentelle, *make the strongest statement by inviting onlookers to behold the home within, rather than by shielding it from view.*

RIGHT: *Gargoyles such as this can be seen on churches in the French countryside, as well as on some grand country homes that sport Gothic styling. Although they appear to be nothing more than fanciful embellishments, gargoyles were actually designed to serve as practical drainage spouts. These fantastic figures were thought to embody fallen angels who were being given a second chance to redeem themselves by guarding buildings. The action of water rushing through their spouts was said to wash away evil.*

RIGHT: *Stone houses dating back centuries are found in the celebrated wine-producing area of Bordeaux. Here, a stately home rests atop the hill, its unadorned façade emphasizing its simple grandeur. Nestled into the hillside below is a smaller cottage-style residence, graced with exuberant foliage and vines. Adding a sense of warm welcome is a planter bursting with colorful blooms set upon the wrought-iron balcony.*

LEFT: *Already flanked by old white shutters and luxurious leafy vines, the windows in this master's house, or* maison de maître, *are given an additional decorative boost by window boxes filled with vibrant bougainvillea. A skillful use of dark and light materials provides soft contrast between the roof, graced with tiny dormers, and the commanding stonework.*

RIGHT: *Located in a small village, this stone house was built close to its neighbors, a tradition that developed partly because of space constraints and also for security reasons. Stone was always favored over timber when available, and the irregular sizes and shapes—no two stones alike—lend an air of individuality.*

OPPOSITE: *Breton blue, a favorite color in Brittany because of the area's many boating and fishing activities, is used on the shutters, window trim, front door, and wooden gate of this home. Only a side door boasts a deep brick red. Both hues enhance the exterior by enlivening the whitewashed façade.*

Getting away from the big city and finding refuge in the country is just as much a French phenomenon as it is an American one, and the choice of weekend abodes takes many forms. For example, a tiny half-timbered Alsatian house (RIGHT) set deep in the woods offers the desired change of pace with its sloping roofline and the privacy provided by its massive stone walls set with relatively few small windows. Another family's preferred getaway is a small stone cottage in Auvergne (BELOW). Quaint dormered windows, stones bearing different hues, and a secluded location create the appeal of this retreat.

ABOVE: *Espaliers have long been a popular gardening device, creating wonderful decorative effects within a fairly small amount of space. From a central vertical stem attached to the wall of a house, branches are trained to grow sideways in tidy rows. Sometimes, the branches yield apples and pears, other times fragrant flowers. Here, an espalier growing against the side wall of a brick home fans out its greenery and red bouquets of color.*

ABOVE: *Whether stopping for a drink at a Parisian café or relaxing at a country home, the French favor taking their meals outdoors, capturing the best view for enjoyment. Here is proof that they know how to set as elegant a table in the fresh outdoors as they do within their homes. All they need are favorite candlesticks, white china, simple crystal, and light-toned linens.* Bon appetit.

ABOVE: *Though the walls were constructed from rough stone, which has been washed with a pale yellow hue, and the door was made of crude wood, the owners of this barn still felt it important to leave a personal touch by carving a tiny heart in one door panel and fronting it with an exuberant garden of tulips and lilacs.*

RIGHT: *Grapes are an important crop in France, and the process of producing wine is a time-consuming labor. In spring new vines are planted; in summer they are tended; and in autumn the grapes are picked, crushed, and fermented. Just as no two grapes are alike, neither are two "high houses," or maisons en hauteur, prevalent in the provinces where wine is made. These centuries-old structures were designed to have the upstairs serve as living quarters, while the ground level would serve as a wine store. Originally a Mediterranean innovation, the style quickly caught on in Burgundy, Provence, and Languedoc.*

RIGHT: *In Provence, a palette of warm, earthy hues made from the oxides in the local sand are used to embellish the homes. Shutters and trims are often painted in contrast-ing colors, and the overall effect is both picture-pretty and quite polished despite the simplicity of the structures. Here is a perfect example of the magic wrought by this practice: with just a piece of faience and a simple lace shawl, a cottage in Provence looks elegantly turned out thanks to its already exquisite façade.*

Multipaned windows that extend down to the
floor but are used like doors to gain access
to or exit from a room are known as French
windows and can be dressed up or down to suit
a residence. The windows on a countryside
chateau in France (ABOVE) sport louvered doors,
while those on a limestone farmhouse (RIGHT) are
framed with rustic slat shutters. In either case,
flowers add a great deal of charm to the façade.

LEFT AND ABOVE: *Many farmhouses in the provinces were built of limestone rubble, with granite framing stones and simple wood plank shutters and doors. Such drab materials left residences looking quite somber, a situation easily remedied in summer months with foliage. With the addition of simple boxes filled with flowers, these two farmhouses in Auvergne go from pallid to picturesque.*

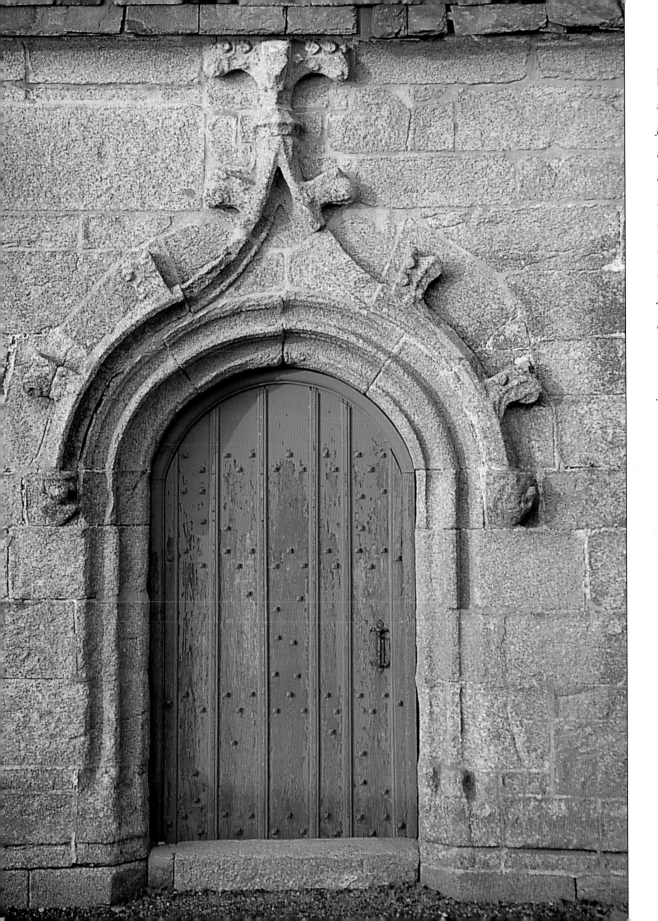

LEFT: *Renaissance-style carvings are found on manors and religious monuments throughout lower Brittany, where granite was frequently used to build homes. Here the moldings and jambs are still perfectly intact on a sixteenth-century Breton manor, framing a massive oak door that was the standard of the day (it was supplanted by framed versions in the seventeenth century). While the dusty red hue seems like an authentic touch, the door was a rich honey color when it was first built and was repainted to suit twentieth-century taste.*

LEFT, TOP: *In Normandy, windows boasting two rows of small panes typically appear in pairs with a structural post dividing them. Thanks to such detailing, they are charming in their own right. In this half-timbered house, the windows need no further adornment than a mass of red flowers.*

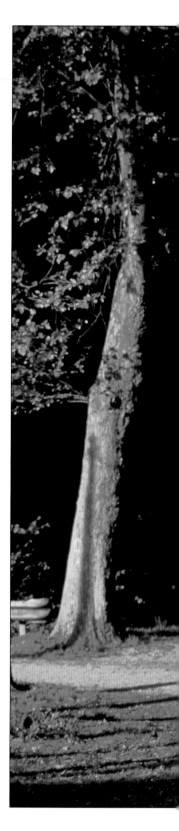

LEFT, BOTTOM: *With its swirling lines and heart-shaped designs, this wrought-iron gate creates a welcoming entrance filled with old-fashioned charm. A delicate praying angel offers a sense of reassurance, as she seems to keep watch over those within the farmhouse. Further evidence of hospitality is seen in the house number, which has been lovingly stenciled in blue and white to stand out against the gray stone and hence can be seen easily by visitors.*

RIGHT: *Home sweet home. At the end of a long gravel driveway lined with shade-providing trees, the sight of home—in this case a turreted château, the French equivalent of a large country home—is a welcome visage.*

CHAPTER TWO
ROOMS FOR LIVING

While the archetypal French country living room of today is a charming space outfitted with all the right trappings, it is actually a rather recent innovation. Until the nineteenth century, many French living quarters (save for the communal abodes that sheltered multigenerational families in parts of southern and eastern France) consisted of only one or two rooms.

The one room that these homes were sure to have was the *salle*, which served as a sort of kitchen-cum–living room. All the activities of a household—from cooking and eating to gathering around the fire and sleeping—took place in the *salle*. If a home was divided into two rooms, the second was a sparsely furnished bedroom, or *chambre*, which was often located to the side of the *salle* or under the eaves of the attic.

Yet despite the limited number of rooms, many newly restored cottages and farmhouses in France sport stunning living rooms, loaded with architectural details and striking pieces of furniture that reflect the provincial style. So where did these special spaces come from?

Most were once living quarters for the family livestock. Households kept their valuable animals on the ground floors of their homes and lived either above them or off to one end of the structure. As animals were slowly evicted from these spaces, the rooms underwent a series of upgrades until they ended up as the sort of living rooms we know today. Other living rooms (especially those with hearths) originated as *salles* and were converted to their present incarnations when a contemporary kitchen was added on to the home.

The architectural elements of these rooms—beamed ceilings, timbered fittings, and stone floors—have been somewhat refurbished to ensure structural safety but have been left primarily intact to retain their rustic charm. Massive limestone hearths, which were often hidden behind newer walls as cottages were modernized over the years, have been unearthed, restored, and enhanced with every sort of fireplace accessory. Although these spacious rooms are not always filled

OPPOSITE: *There is no need to sacrifice high style in the French countryside. Here, simple pieces are paired together for a country version of Empire styling, exuding the same sort of symmetrical balance and glamour found in that type of decor. But the vignette also retains an aura of earthiness thanks to the cunning way in which design elements of the Empire period, such as gilt trim and yellow walls, have been manipulated; gilt is seen here only in small doses (on the mirror, the pulls of the commode, and the rims of the topiary pots), and the walls are mellow instead of bold.*

with strictly provincial furnishings, they certainly include enough of these kinds of pieces to create a French country ambience.

Achieving this look in a contemporary room can be as simple as incorporating a massive provincial armoire, some lace curtains, or a few Louis XV–inspired banquettes into the decor. Or, the architectural bones of a room can be manipulated to create the desired mood. Installing a French country–style beamed ceiling, a large stone hearth with copper accessories, or a tiled floor will do the trick. Regardless of which route is chosen, the result will be the same: the room will be imbued with classic French country charm.

BELOW: *Like a crusty old cauldron brimming with all sorts of tasty ingredients, this antiquated space is filled with a wide range of appealing pieces. Shapely and light, these pieces cast their sunny dispositions upon the room, preventing the massive dark Gothic architecture from making the space seem archaic. A blue fleur-de-lis pattern stenciled on the chalk white walls, along with checkered upholstery in the same shades, provides a cheery counterpoint to the dank-looking limestone cornices and hearth and gives the space its French country spark.*

ABOVE: *Since a hearth is the heart of many a French home, clever decorating devices were enlisted to suggest a fireplace in this country living room. Now a stylized version, complete with a faux mantel created by cornice molding, is the focal point of the space. But it is actually the matched pair of classic eighteenth-century settees, complete with rush seats, that gives the room its French country aura. Pillows and curtains made out of traditional Provençal fabrics (patterned after the printed cottons originally imported to France from India in the seventeenth century) and a Kashmir shawl covering the coffee table further imbue the room with unusual authenticity.*

OPPOSITE: *Since hearths are such an important and beautiful part of regional style in France, country kitchens are often turned into living rooms when homes are rehabbed. Here, a typical fireplace in Brittany, which was clearly once the functional center of a kitchen, has become the dramatic focal point of a sitting room. The hearth is surrounded by a hodgepodge of local pieces collected by the homeowners, and it is warmed up with a new floor that boasts a traditional pattern, covering the cold antiquated flagstones underneath.*

ABOVE: *A once humble country space becomes a bit more highbrow by playing on its natural attributes. The imposing open fireplace, edged with dressed stones, used to be the center of the original kitchen before the space was transformed into a living room. Now surrounded by pieces that have a polished country appeal, such as a posh winged chair, a sumptuous sofa, and a gleaming ladder-back chair, the fireplace takes on an air of grandeur.*

LEFT: *A cavernous living room in an old country home in France becomes downright cozy thanks to an array of French antiques that come from a variety of periods. An ornate eighteenth-century marble mantel and a gilt mirror anchor the room while helping to cut the ceiling height down to size. Meanwhile, a whimsical play on symmetry draws the eye toward such fabulous matching decorative elements as the torchères, sconces, Deco chairs, and pieces of pottery, thereby diverting attention away from the excess of space and rendering the setting more intimate.*

RIGHT: *Do not be deceived by the apparent simplicity of a country tableau. Here, the chalky white tones of a coarse plaster wall and rugged hearth are enriched by a seemingly casual, but actually carefully planned, arrangement of accents in rich hues of blue. The accessories, which include refined pieces of Chinoiserie pottery, rustic seascapes, and a modest wood chair, strike just the right balance to give the setting a polished but still provincial appeal.*

RIGHT: *A mantel in a modest French country cottage goes from mundane to magnificent when it is used as a topiary form. The gilt-edged mirror and matching urns add a touch of glamour to the setting, balancing the earthy ambience prompted by the foliage and lending an air of elegance to the funky approach.*

LEFT: *An innovative use of pattern is responsible for the casual yet cosmopolitan elegance of this living room in the South of France. While the scheme appears at first glance to be quite bold and forthright, it actually demonstrates subtle variations, for there are different types of stripes on the sofa, chairs, and walls. As these elements play off one another, they create the illusion of cohesiveness.*

ABOVE: *Although this living room in a French country home sports all the touches of a formal decor, the features have been relaxed a bit to fit the locale. The damask sofa is overstuffed enough to be comfortably casual, while a typical Provençal cotton print makes a stately Louis XV bergère seem less intimidating and far more inviting. A traditional soft yellow hue warms up the entire space.*

ABOVE: *Provincial furnishings were made by anonymous craftsmen in every region of France, often reflecting the distinctive styles of their period. But precise dating is difficult because some forms, such as the domed cherry Louis XV armoire in this sitting room, were popular and continued to be made in the provinces long after the specific style fell out of favor in Parisian workrooms. As this cabinet clearly shows, a piece of this scale can have a major impact on an entire room.*

RIGHT: *The adventurous use of color can make a traditional space seem far more engaging. Here, deep azure, the shade of the sky right after sunset, gives a sense of drama to what is for the most part a fairly traditional country room. Another novel touch is the mixing of contemporary pieces with such French provincial elements as classic ladder-back armchairs, Empire fauteuil, and a Regency corner cabinet.*

RIGHT: *Sometimes, just one powerful detail can imbue a room with a specific flavor. These vibrant curtains made of a hand-blocked Provençal cotton give a huge dose of French country styling to a plain window in a city apartment. Coupled with a simple metal window box filled with flowers of a similar hue, the curtains help to create a vignette that is far more dynamic than the individual components.*

Regardless of pedigree, when similar objects are gathered together en masse, the sum is greater than the parts. Here, two tableaux from French country homes—one created from ordinary vases filled with freshly cut flowers (LEFT) and the other from antique decanters and a tea caddy (ABOVE)—illustrate the point. Despite the fact that they are in the midst of rustic surroundings, these vignettes demonstrate the chic savoir faire for which the French are renowned. Both settings are bathed in sunny yellow, a color that not only has a history of tradition in the French country-side, but can add warmth and depth to any style of room.

LEFT: *The travails that befall a structure in the French countryside are rarely repaired; instead, these imperfections become prized parts of the decor. Thus, the missing paneling from a limestone hearth and the damaged area above a door frame where a cornice once rested are seen as signs of character rather than as shortcomings. Together, they contribute to the ambience and integrity of the residence.*

RIGHT: *The nooks and crannies of this secretary have been mined to display a charming collection of Limoges boxes, plus a few larger pieces of traditional tole. While these classics are right at home on the Louis XVI piece, virtually any antique desk or cabinet can acquire a French country tone when accessorized with provincial collectibles.*

LEFT: *Formal French furnishings can be equally at home in the countryside. Here, a Louis XV sofa, covered with pillows inspired by Aubusson tapestries, anchors a distinctly Victorian living room in a country home. The piece works well with the eclectic elements of the room, which range from floridly romantic statues of angels to Gothic Revival lamps.*

ABOVE: *Reproduction fabrics and furnishings can be used to evoke a French country feeling. The flowery print of this chintz was inspired by the prints of Provence, while the detailing of the carved armoire takes its cues from the provincial pieces of the eighteenth century.*

The trappings of grand country living, such as intricate wall treatments,
elaborate hearths, and beautiful wood and stone floors, take center stage in
these living rooms in the French countryside. Although one room (RIGHT) is
purely Louis XV and the other (ABOVE) is a romantic milieu that borrows from
many periods, both spaces contain fine examples of French antiques. But
thanks to the comfortably lived-in looks of the furnishings and the obvious
signs of wear and tear on the hearths, the rooms also radiate rustic spirit.
Like elegant outfits that should be worn instead of stored away in a closet,
lavish spaces seem far less pretentious when they are used every day.

CHAPTER THREE

THE COMMUNAL KITCHEN

Throughout French history, good food and drink have been raised to the level of art, which is why the kitchen has been not only a place to prepare meals, but a forerunner of today's heart-of-the-home room. Here, food is prepared, meals are savored, and people join together for sustenance of both the spirit and stomach.

Because the communal kitchen has traditionally served all these functions—and still does today—it has needed to include areas for cooking and cleaning as well as for eating and gathering. Whether these spaces remain distinct or are melded together depends to a large degree on the room's square footage.

Stylistically, there is great latitude in the choice of materials, colors, and design styles. However, the architecture of the home, the furnishings used in other rooms, and the age-old traditions passed down through the various provinces provide the greatest incentive for one kitchen to take on the charm of a Brittany farmhouse and another the splendor of a Loire Valley château.

Several features appear more frequently and have become almost trademarks of the French communal kitchen. A working fireplace was originally an essential because it provided the home's main source of heat. Today, many homes still have a large hearth—sometimes functional, sometimes decorative—as well as a mantel and walk-in–size alcove.

Generous storage is also characteristic of the French country kitchen. Pieces range from richly carved *dressoirs*, *vaisseliers* (cabinets or dressers with shelves), *buffets-bas* (waist-high cupboards used as sideboards), *panetières* (intricately shaped and carved cupboards for storing bread), and armoires down to simple slabs for shelves and unadorned cabinets. Some owners prefer to keep everything within view; others like to conceal the contents.

A large table and comfortable seating are critical elements for eating and lingering in the communal kitchen. The most common setup consists of an unadorned rectangular wooden farmhouse-style table surrounded by rush-bottomed ladder-back chairs, appearing sometimes in an assortment of styles.

OPPOSITE: *Knowing the superb culinary skills of the French, it is easy to understand why they have tradtionally coveted copper pots. Most households had collections of such cookware, which would be hung on racks because storage space was minimal. Arrayed in this manner, the pots were out of the way yet always within reach.*

Rustic earthy materials—the most popular being brick, wood, stone, and terra-cotta—are used in a variety of shapes and sizes to line kitchen walls, floors, and countertops. These elements offer age-old elegance as well as practicality.

And last but not least, pot racks (known as *crémaillères*) are integral components of the communal kitchen, having had a long and fruitful history in the French countryside. Along with the requisite copper pots that dangle from them, these highly practical elements also make beautiful, gleaming decorative accessories.

RIGHT: *This contemporary kitchen pays clever and indisputable homage to French country styling. The hard-wearing black-and-white tile floor, laid in a bold diamond pattern, is linoleum instead of clay, and the requisite baker's rack has been replaced by high-tech stainless steel industrial shelves to provide open storage. But the most prized elements of the French country kitchen remain perfectly intact, such as pots suspended from the ceiling and burnished walls rubbed with an earthy-colored hue.*

RIGHT: *A kitchen emanating a French country feeling does not necessarily have to sport anything specifically French in style. Here, a British Aga cooker, which heats food as well as the home's water system, serves as an anchor. Displays of pots and dried flowers lend a true country feeling to the space. But the ornately patterned tiles used in the backsplash, along with a set of intricately embellished chairs caned in colored stripes, give the kitchen the kind of panache that says French country.*

ABOVE: *Prized copper pots hang like medals on a wall in this French country kitchen, which boasts an elegant hodgepodge of furnishings achieved through years of tasteful, and heartfelt, accumulating. The wood pieces warm up the flagstone floor and contrast with the intricately enameled cast-iron wood-burning stove traditionally used for warming winter soups and stews. Note the elegant glasses and decanter on the table, which show that entertaining is one of the many activities that take place in this multifaceted room.*

OPPOSITE:

Thanks to similarities in shape, scale, and condition, a medley of ruggedly disparate pieces creates sweet harmony in the eating area of this French country kitchen. The armoire and decorative door bear characteristics of different provinces but are unified by their height, while the traditional slat-style garden chairs and a walnut dining table are equally overscale. All the pieces in the room display bold angles and possess the same raw-boned feeling brought on by years of beloved use.

RIGHT: *Even breakfast takes on a festive mood in a kitchen where the dichotomy between fancy and plain is palpable. The antique table and characteristically mismatched chairs are simple in style and made of the most basic wood. Nonetheless, silver and pressed linen napkins adorn the table, giving the room a slightly dressy air. More favorite platters, pitchers, bowls, and cups are displayed on the shelves above the built-in buffet.*

ABOVE: *Cooking and entertaining are frequent rather than novel events among most French families, which explains why their kitchens are often designed with row upon row of open shelving laden with bowls, platters, casserole dishes, and other culinary necessities. While practical, the contents also make for an attractive display. In this kitchen, where preparations for a party are under way, everything is within arm's reach, including pitchers, canisters, and some wooden spoons, forks, and a rolling pin crammed into an old jar.*

LEFT: *Used as a crucial ingredient in many dishes and imbibed during family and company meals, wine is just as integral a part of the French country kitchen as are appliances, cookware, food, and utensils. In the corner of such a kitchen, far enough from the sources of heat so that the contents are not endangered, sits a simple, painted-blue farmhouse rack that houses the family's stash. The bottles have been lovingly collected through the years and gingerly laid on their sides to age.*

RIGHT: *In this inviting kitchen, ceramic tiles sporting a shade of blue that is reminiscent of the Mediterranean on a sunny day line the backsplash, create an easy-to-clean resting spot for food and utensils, and adorn the hood of the stove. Other characteristically French country elements include a pot rack with heavy copper pots and saucepans, handcrafted wooden cabinetry, a framed fruit print, an old hanging lamp, and a cherished white porcelain stove that has been in the family for decades.*

LEFT: *Kitchens are for relaxing as well as for eating and cooking. In this large multipurpose kitchen, a small recess in the stone wall proved the perfect place for a banquette. Upholstered in a geometric blue-and-white fabric, the piece echoes the collection of faience above. The white metal bread box, a modern twist on the traditional wood panetière carved to store bread, was included more as a whimsical decorative touch than as a practical place for safekeeping fresh baguettes.*

OPPOSITE: *Traditional furnishings that would look just as proper in a living room or dining room are used in French country kitchens to add dignity as well as to provide practical services. Here, a long pine buffet with drawers and a bottom shelf adds charm while housing cookbooks. The piece mixes well with a walnut china rack that displays a favorite collection of faience and Chinese-inspired dessert plates and cups. Baskets for plants and bread contribute to the casual ambience, as does the border paper, which boasts a simple cornucopia motif.*

BELOW: *In the spirit of a typical French country kitchen, this space includes a variety of materials, styles, and proportions that combine to create an eclectic whole, causing the room to appear as though it evolved through the years. Moreover, various specific elements of French country styling have been integrated into the cabinetry: the center island manifests deep carving typical of Normandy, and the spindled plate guards on the corner unit are taken from the dressoirs of Brittany. The cabinetry, beams, floorboards, table, chairs, and stools bring in a wide range of woods, while the green marble on the island acts as an elegant contemporary foil.*

LEFT: *Aside from the pot rack, nothing epitomizes quintessential French style like the baker's rack, which is used for storage and display. Here, a baker's rack made of wrought iron and brass shows off an eclectic collection of objets d'art, plants, and wine in a kitchen that has been handsomely papered in two distinct fabrics sharing the common denominator of a blue-and-white color scheme. Both designs—large checks and a toile de Jouy—are equally representative of French country style and are never passé.*

BELOW: *In this corner of a French country kitchen, French ladder-back armchairs with rush seats are grouped around a plain wood table that has been dressed up with a handsome white linen cloth. A fireplace graced by a wooden mantel, as well as a cloth frill twisted across the opening to give the chimney draw and prevent soot from darkening the wall, offers visual warmth while the fire within provides comfort on cold winter days. A nearby built-in floor-to-ceiling cabinet stores dishes and other items for table settings.*

ABOVE: *An attractive still life with a French country flavor can be fashioned from such simple elements as a big bouquet of fresh flowers placed in front of bottles of oil, vinegar, and flavored liqueurs. And the best part of the arrangement is that it can change frequently, bringing something new to the kitchen on a regular basis.*

RIGHT: *An imposing eighteenth-century walnut vaisselier from Brittany features the province's classic spindled plate guards. With its deep red painted back, the piece provides a dramatic resting spot for a collection of different Limoges china dinner plates. Adding more personality to the scene are a large glass vase of fresh flowers and a generous soup tureen, the latter of which is also from Limoges.*

BELOW: *This ceiling, with its joists supported by and embedded in the tops of the beams, is so characteristic of the French farmhouse that the style is referred to as à la française. Although the rest of the kitchen is not specifically French, the ceiling sets an overwhelmingly French tone. Herbs dangling from old recycled beams at the tops of some of the windows contribute to this feeling, as does the selection of rustic materials, including the brick used to face the cabinet that houses a cooktop and oven.*

ABOVE: *An important part of life in the French countryside has been drying herbs and flowers, a craft that is still being practiced today in this kitchen. Together with collections of kitchen utensils and various odds and ends, the dried herbs and flowers make the space come alive in a crowded yet appealing way. Small wrought-iron skillets, old knives, and other kitchen bric-a-brac adorn the brick wall beside the now purely decorative fireplace, which is currently home to some brass and copper tea kettles. Heavy ceramic jugs, once filled with wine but now only ornamental, rest peacefully on the floor.*

BELOW: *The spirit of this eat-in kitchen resonates with an American country feeling on account of its wooden walls, flooring, and door, along with its simple painted furnishings. However, the space does boast some distinctly French touches, including a large tin pail filled with dried flowers and the mixing of pieces of furniture painted in different hues.*

ABOVE: *An old stone farmhouse kitchen with a restored open timbered ceiling has been modernized for a family that likes to cook, though the room still retains its country feeling. The roof has been opened with skylights; a two-level center island was constructed to offer distinct spaces for cooking and cleaning; and a wooden table and chair have been added to provide another place for labor-intensive cooking chores. Irregularly shaped flagstones line the floor, helping to visually unify the kitchen's many textures, materials, and subtle wood tones.*

RIGHT: *In a small landscaped courtyard off a kitchen, a former butcher's table has been topped by festive blue-and-white tiles, transforming it into a place to enjoy a game of dominoes and some wine on a pleasant afternoon. The Breton blue color scheme is carried through in the painted chair (brought outdoors from the kitchen) and lovely cut crystal goblets that seem almost too good to be used outdoors.*

RIGHT: *Touches of French country styling permeate this kitchen, which has a decidedly dressy instead of typically casual demeanor. The Provençal-inspired tablecloth has been deepened for a richer look; the white country lace curtains have been gussied up with shirring; and the traditional pot rack has been relegated to an out-of-the-way alcove.*

BELOW: *In this quaint kitchen, pale pine faces all the cabinetry, which is enhanced by both delicately patterned and solid blues. Square blue-and-white tiles in two patterns line the backsplash, echoing the collection of plates that accent the area above the windows. Further splashes of blue include the painted window casements and chairs. Even the hand towel boasts a blue-and-white Provençal design.*

ABOVE: *As in many French kitchens, the china—or at least a large portion of it—is perpetually on display. The almost all white background of this room adds a crisp freshness and timeless appeal, also typical of Scandinavian design.*

LEFT: *Rows of hardworking copper cookware and a long trestle table make this French country kitchen appropriate for a large family that entertains frequently. But it is the beamed ceiling that gives the space its authenticity. Other rustic elements, such as the fireplace and the stone floor, inspired the owners to refrain from painting over the wall's rough stucco finish. Adjacent to the double range is an old stone country sink, which is useful for filling pots.*

RIGHT, TOP: *A limestone-and-tile sink, decked in traditional blue and white, was the inspiration for the striking blue shade of paint used on these walls. A built-in wall cupboard, set off from the rest of the room with a deeper hue, provides space-efficient storage in the small kitchen, which receives natural light from a small dormer window.*

RIGHT, BOTTOM: *A fancy Louis XVI–style armchair brings an elegant touch to the casual blue-and-white cotton skirted table at one end of a small kitchen. The painted blue window frame adds more color and eliminates the need for curtains so that the lush landscape outdoors is always in view.*

ABOVE: *The old-style French kitchen frequently becomes a beehive of activity, as evidenced by this room. Atop the tiled counter, fresh greenery is readied for use in a centerpiece; a lower counter is covered with fresh vegetables that will be made into a salad; and the ledge above the stove is crammed end-to-end with jars of preserves and pickled vegetables. Copper cookware decorates the walls, while blue-and-white pottery and tiles provide refreshing color. The recycled wooden gate, a charming reminder of the home's farmhouse origins, leads into the living room beyond.*

RIGHT: *The eating area in this French country cottage kitchen demonstrates the wonders of the simpler things in life. A bouquet of colorful garden flowers in an old tub, a rustic wooden plank table that coordinates beautifully with the kitchen walls, and fetching painted-blue chairs that add a welcome splash of color create a wonderful spot for a tête-à-tête that is just as appealing as a much grander setting. An assortment of old stainless steel utensils hanging on the wall brings additional panache to the setup.*

BELOW: *Large cast-iron cookers, now defunct, anchor this simply furnished room, the windows of which were deliberately left uncurtained to contribute to the no-nonsense ambience. Above the cooking area, an assortment of tiles is configured to resemble a piece of artwork. These tiles, along with similar ones lining the dado and big copper pots and earthenware casually arranged on shelves and against walls, are the prime sources of color in the decor. Simple ladder-back chairs and an absolutely plain rectangular wooden table occupy the center of the space, creating a good work surface as well as a fine place to dine.*

BELOW: *Tall topiary bushes stand guard at the end of a dining table in a kitchen that is classically French and casually chic with its stone arch, overhead beams, and pine table and ladder-back chairs. Distinguishing the host from the rest of the diners, a tapestry-covered wing chair is positioned at the head of the table, where it adds an air of importance. A simple armoire with a nonetheless commanding presence stands tall and proud nearby, making dining essentials easily accessible.*

BELOW: *With a typically French sleight of hand, a decrepit old clock in the room shown at left is transformed into an attention grabber. Framed with a hand-painted border and topped with a slew of dried roses, it becomes an architectural element rather than a mere antique.*

ABOVE: *In this elegant château, the kitchen was designed to look like and function as a space meant more for romantic old-world entertaining than cooking. Nevertheless, all the necessary appliances are present, though a bit camouflaged by wonderful old materials and paint finishes. The walls of the room were frescoed and painted to resemble wood paneling, with the insets a subtle blue-gray, ringed by the palest taupe and an antique gold. Blending in harmoniously with the color scheme, terra-cotta tiles line the floor and mirror the color of the painted ceiling. Even the accessories reflect old-world styling, including a painted Louis XV chair, an elegant damask tablecloth, and dried flowers turned upside down to fill a former hood.*

CHAPTER FOUR

ROOMS FOR RETREAT

Bedrooms, at least as we now know them, were rarely found before the nineteenth century in the French countryside, where the habit of sleeping by the fire in the *salle* was widespread. Any bedrooms that did exist were used to house the girls of a family, and such spaces were sparsely furnished with merely a bed or two and a simple wardrobe.

Loft-style sleeping alcoves under the rafters were more common for those not sleeping by the fire. Eventually, many of these were adapted to become entire rooms. This evolution led to the quintessential French country bedroom tucked away under the pitched beamed ceilings of a provincial cottage.

Since the bedroom (if a household was wealthy enough to have one) was a communal space, provincial beds were constructed so as to provide privacy as well as warmth. Many were draped with hangings so the occupants could dress without being seen. These textiles also performed the helpful duties of keeping out dust, dirt, bugs, and cold air.

As the wealth of a household increased, so too did the beauty of its beds. Most were at least four feet (122cm) wide, designed to accommodate two occupants. The beds had thick mattresses made of straw or, in wealthier homes, feathers, and they were topped with large feather quilts and homemade sheets and blankets. Because they were usually placed against a wall or in an alcove, they were heavily carved on one side and plainly finished on the other.

Different types of beds became popular in different regions of France. High box beds (*lits-clos*), totally enclosed by wooden panels that were often richly carved and colorfully painted, were prominent in Brittany, Normandy, Auvergne, and parts of the Alps. (In the Alps, sheep slept underneath them, serving as bedwarmers.)

Beds with canopies attached to the bedposts or suspended from the ceilings, running the gamut from full overhangs to half-testers, prevailed throughout all the provinces but reflected regional differences. Angel beds (*lits d'ange*) with four short posts, a plain headboard, no footboard, and half-testers were commonplace in the South, as were *litoches* (the same bed sans the hangings). Elegantly draped beds with full canopies totally concealing the mattress were referred to as *à la duchesse* and could often be found in the North, where the colder climate dictated a more enclosed space.

OPPOSITE: *Despite the fact that these furnishings are pure Louis XV, they look right at home in this French country residence. Though once formal and grand, they now radiate a faded glory that comes from years, perhaps generations, of use. The aura of warmth and comfort is further evoked by the slightly decayed trompe l'oeil paint finishes on the headboard and nightstand and the faded Aubusson-inspired fabrics.*

Creating a French country bedroom today is often as simple as outfitting a room with an ornate bed topped with a canopy of some configuration or a simple bed covered with a traditional provincial textile, such as a *boutis* (an intricately quilted, brightly colored coverlet of Provençal design) or a hand-worked white lace spread. Add a wardrobe, be it simple or elaborate, a coffer, and perhaps a few comfortable country chairs, and *voilà*—the French country bedroom is reborn.

BELOW: *Heavy snow white linens alter the look of this bedroom in a French country home. The dark* lit en bateau *goes from simple to stunning thanks to the pristine spread, while curtains transform the area around the bed into an intimate alcove. A delicate row of lace trim on the bottom of the drapes along with satin cording and tassels keep the textiles from seeming too austere. Meanwhile, a subtle Provençal-style flower pattern on the walls imbues the room with just a hint of color.*

LEFT: *A dark, masculine Empire-style bed becomes airy and romantic with the right trappings in this French country room. By suspending gauzy white cotton from the ceiling, the bed is transformed into an* alluring lit en baldaquin *(canopy bed). The blue-and-white color scheme gives the room its lively spirit and makes the space seem as though it has been patterned after a set of Chinese-inspired faience from a French village.*

BELOW: *A picture is worth a thousand words, and the stunning* toile de Jouy *that envelops this bedroom radiates the message that this is a stately French room. The traditional fabric originated in Jouy in the mid-eighteenth century and is well known for its large pictorial repeats appearing in a single bold color. The grand aura that such a pattern usually imparts is toned down a bit here with a white linen coverlet and a white ladder-back chair.*

ABOVE: *An eclectic mix of elements adds up to definitive French country style in this attic bedroom. Its charm comes from a blend of fine period pieces of disparate pedigrees, including an Art Nouveau brass bed and an Empire chest, as well as the subtle contrasting color scheme of white and pale gray. The deep earthy hues of the furnishings, which include not only the bed and chest but also a stack of rattan storage cases and an old wooden chair, serve as the unifying element.*

OPPOSITE: *Lace textiles were de rigueur in fashionable European homes during the eighteenth and nineteenth centuries, and were made into curtains, coverlets, and tablecloths. They were particularly adored in the French countryside, almost as much as the hand-blocked floral fabrics of Provence. In this bedroom, a provincial lace coverlet gives the space its French country ambience, though the other furnishings—an Art Nouveau wrought-iron bed and basket and a painted rush-seat chair—are also authentic French country pieces.*

ABOVE: *Box beds, which were enclosed on three sides and shuttered or draped on their fourth edge, were popular in the French countryside for their privacy and capacity to keep out drafts. Outfitted with huge straw mattresses and large feather-filled duvets, they were beautifully carved and sometimes sported painted finishes like the one shown here. Today, they are more romantic than pragmatic, possessing the ability to infuse a contemporary room with a country tone.*

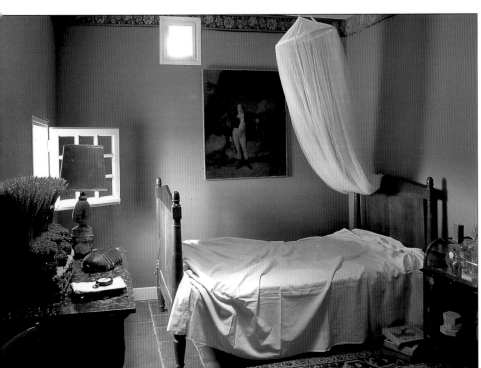

Since clay was abundant in some of the southern French provinces, many homes in those areas had tile floors. These surfaces offered the benefits of being cool in the summer, warm in the winter, and easy to clean year-round. Here, two Provence-inspired bedrooms have such floors, as well as small windows and mosquito netting to keep the heat and bugs at bay. The creative use of some other trappings typical of Provençal interiors, including a border inspired by the fabrics of the region (LEFT) and a traditional boutis (ABOVE), effortlessly imbues these rooms with the flavor of the French countryside.

LEFT: *Often, all it takes is one strong element to bestow a certain style upon a room. The bed in this simply furnished room could be from Sweden or Belgium, and the cream-colored linens with lace edging are ubiquitous throughout Europe. But the charming chair, with its regal gilt finish and an endearing fleur-de-lis emblazoned on its medallion back, is unmistakably Louis XV, thereby giving this otherwise generic country look a French flavor.*

LEFT: *Instead of the furnishings, it is the fabrics and decorative moldings that give this room its romantic country appeal. The exuberant French chintz is used as a duvet and repeated on part of the back wall to simulate a headboard. Cream accents in the molding and pure white linens soften the loftiness of the setting, making it far less formal.*

ABOVE: *Set in an alcove topped with an ornate cornice, a Louis XVI daybed is effectively separated from the rest of the room. Matching fauteuils that face the hearth make it clear that the space does double duty as a sitting room. The two areas are unified by two small Oriental rugs bearing similar hues and by the dramatic shade of red used on the daybed and the chairs' upholstery.*

BELOW: *With the help of a bed crown, a traditional lit d'ange has been recreated in this room. But instead of being draped in opulent tapestries, the bed is graced by a rustic chintz that gives the room its country flavor. Other modest textiles used in unusual ways include a gauzy cotton backdrop for the vanity and translucent window curtains caught with tiebacks and puddled to perfection on the floor.*

ABOVE: *The ambience projected by a simple window dressed in white and accented with a few well-chosen accessories can be sufficient for certain rooms when a spare, rather than overdone or crowded, look is desired. A humble French lace hankie may have served as raw material for these country curtains, but the overall effect of the tableau, which exudes charisma, is anything but plain.*

RIGHT: *This nineteenth-century wrought-iron daybed could be of any origin, but it takes on a distinctly French persona in these surroundings thanks to creamy lace-trimmed linens and the magnificent French windows that lie beyond. Draping these windows with layers of simple billowing cotton instead of something more ornate also contributes to the effect and keeps the tone of the space on track.*

ABOVE: *Outfitted with aged, but not vintage, fixtures, this predominantly white bathroom, or* salle de bain, *is bathed in country appeal thanks to a winsome bucolic mural. Even such refined French antiques as a crystal chandelier, a Louis XVI–style stool, gilt-framed prints, and fancy sconces cannot deprive the space of its rustic grandeur.*

LEFT: *Here, decorative devices derived from French country styling spruce up what otherwise would be considered a fairly plain washroom. A Provençal-inspired floral cotton was used for the balloon shades, the skirt of an old porcelain sink, the liner of the clothing hamper, and the trim of the fauteuil. Note the crisp white lattice work, which masks a thoroughly routine tub, making the cleansing experience in this space somewhat akin to bathing outdoors.*

BELOW: *The vernacular of this Normandy cottage, with its timber detailing and chalky walls, shows up even in the washroom, which was probably a bed chamber when the home was originally built. Because of the strong architectural elements of the room, the furnishings become less important. At the same time, though, certain pieces stand out, including a primitive milking stool, a wicker armchair softened with a large cushion, and a dressy Oriental carpet, all of which assume a country demeanor thanks to the surroundings.*